T0400939

Space Exploration

by Connor Stratton

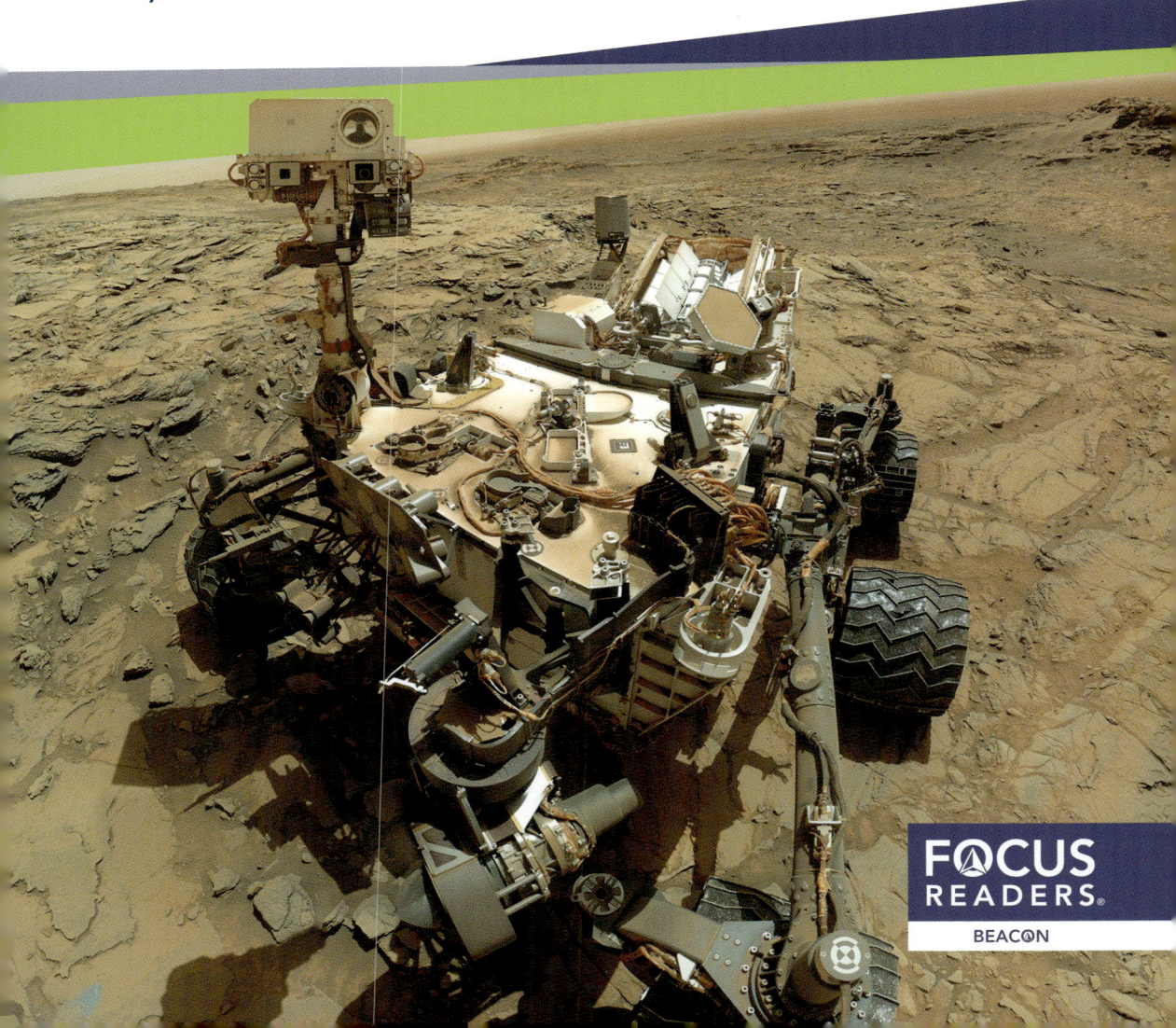

www.focusreaders.com

Focus Readers is distributed by North Star Editions:
sales@northstareditions.com | 888-417-0195

Produced for Focus Readers by Red Line Editorial.

Photographs ©: JPL-Caltech/MSSS/NASA, cover, 1; GSFC/SOHO/NASA, 4; Johns Hopkins APL/NASA, 7; Shutterstock Images, 8, 20, 22; JSC/NASA, 10; Boeing/JSC/NASA, 13, 29; Johns Hopkins University Applied Physics Laboratory/Southwest Research Institute/Roman Tkachenko/NASA, 14–15; Tony Gray and Sandra Joseph/NASA, 16; ESA/JPL/NASA, 19; Bridget Caswell/GRC/NASA, 24; GSFC/NASA, 27

Library of Congress Cataloging-in-Publication Data
Library of Congress Cataloging-in-Publication Data is available on the Library of Congress website.

ISBN
978-1-63739-249-2 (hardcover)
978-1-63739-301-7 (paperback)
978-1-63739-403-8 (ebook pdf)
978-1-63739-353-6 (hosted ebook)

Printed in the United States of America
Mankato, MN
082022

About the Author

Connor Stratton writes and edits nonfiction children's books. When he was younger, he wanted to be an astronaut. When he got glasses in middle school, he realized that dream was unlikely. But writing about space turned out to be pretty rewarding, too.

Table of Contents

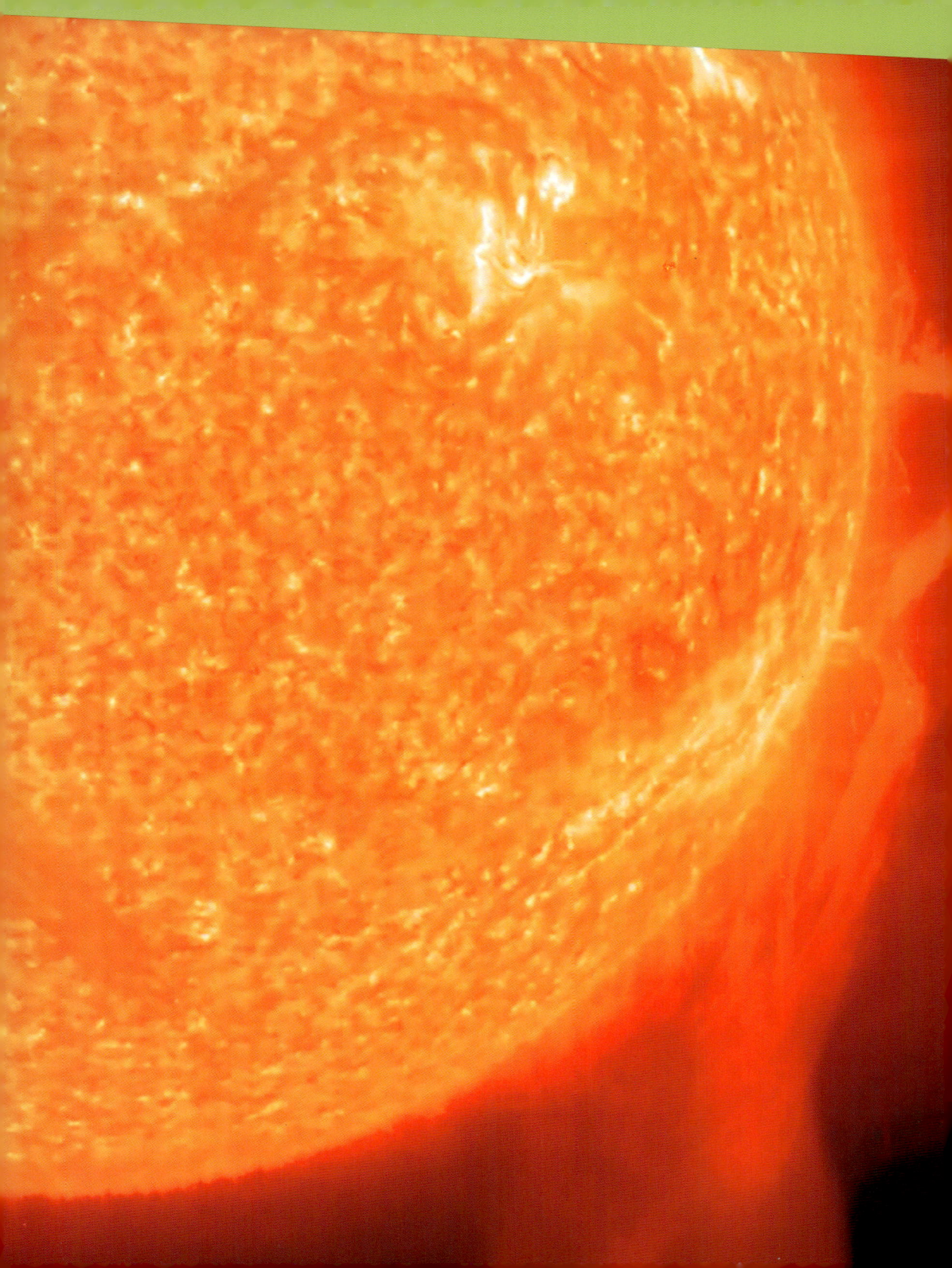

Chapter 1

Parker Solar Probe

In August 2018, the Parker Solar **Probe** blasted into space. It headed toward the Sun. Three months later, the probe set a record. No spacecraft had ever gone closer to the Sun.

 **The Sun is approximately 93 million miles (150 million km) from Earth.**

The probe **orbited** the Sun many times. It also set another record. It became the fastest spacecraft in history. The probe reached speeds of more than 330,000 miles per hour (532,000 km/h).

The Parker Solar Probe gathered **data**. Scientists learned about the Sun's outer **atmosphere**. This

Did You Know?

Objects near the Sun get very hot. So, the Parker Solar Probe used a thick shield.

 Scientists expected the probe to go within 3.83 million miles (6.16 million km) of the Sun.

area is called the corona. The probe's trip showed the value of exploring space.

Chapter 2

History of Exploring Space

People have always looked at the night sky. At first, people explored space with their eyes. In the 1600s, scientists made the first **telescopes**. These tools helped find new planets and moons.

 **In 1610, Galileo Galilei used a telescope and discovered that Jupiter had moons.**

 **Astronaut Edwin "Buzz" Aldrin walks on the Moon in 1969.**

In the 1900s, scientists developed spaceflight. They built rockets. They built probes, too.

The first spacecraft left Earth in 1957. Four years later, the first person went to space. And in 1969, **astronauts** landed on the Moon.

Scientists continued to explore. Probes flew past other planets. By 1989, a probe had visited Neptune. That is the most distant planet.

The 1990s brought even more discoveries. Scientists sent a large telescope into space. It was called the Hubble Space Telescope. It helped study faraway objects.

In 1997, a **rover** explored Mars. It was the first rover on another planet. A few years later, people also began living in space. Astronauts built the International Space Station. Many astronauts visited over the years. They worked on science projects in space.

Did You Know?

In 2001, a spacecraft landed on an asteroid for the first time. An asteroid is a rocky object that is smaller than a planet.

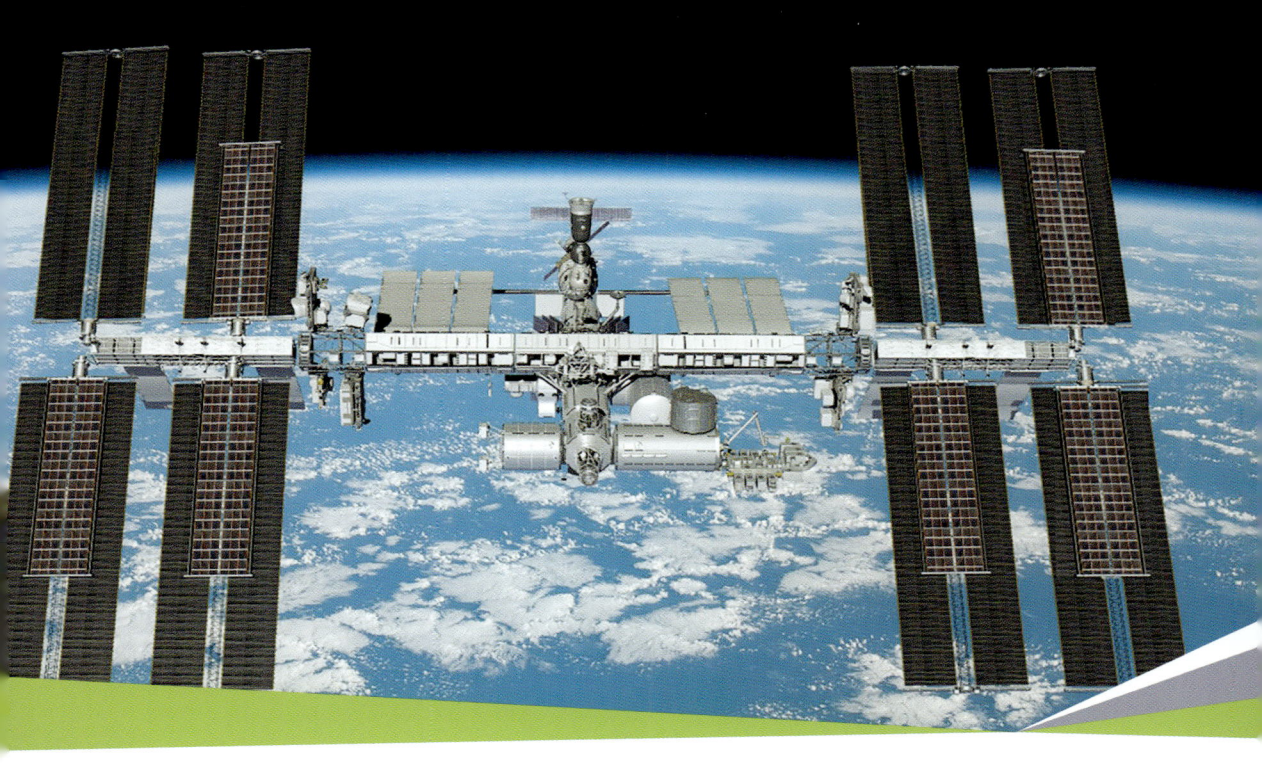

 By the end of 2021, more than 250 people had been to the International Space Station.

Meanwhile, spacecraft kept traveling. In 2012, a probe left the **solar system**. People learned a lot from these journeys. They also learned how much there still was to discover.

New Horizons

Until 2015, no spacecraft had flown near Pluto. This **dwarf planet** is very far from Earth. It is in the Kuiper Belt. This area lies beyond Neptune. It is made up of many icy objects.

In 2015, the New Horizons probe reached Pluto. The probe took up-close pictures of Pluto. It gathered information about Pluto's atmosphere.

New Horizons kept flying. It moved through the Kuiper Belt. In 2020, the probe flew past Arrokoth. This icy rock is the farthest object ever visited.

Arrokoth is approximately 22 miles (35 km) long.

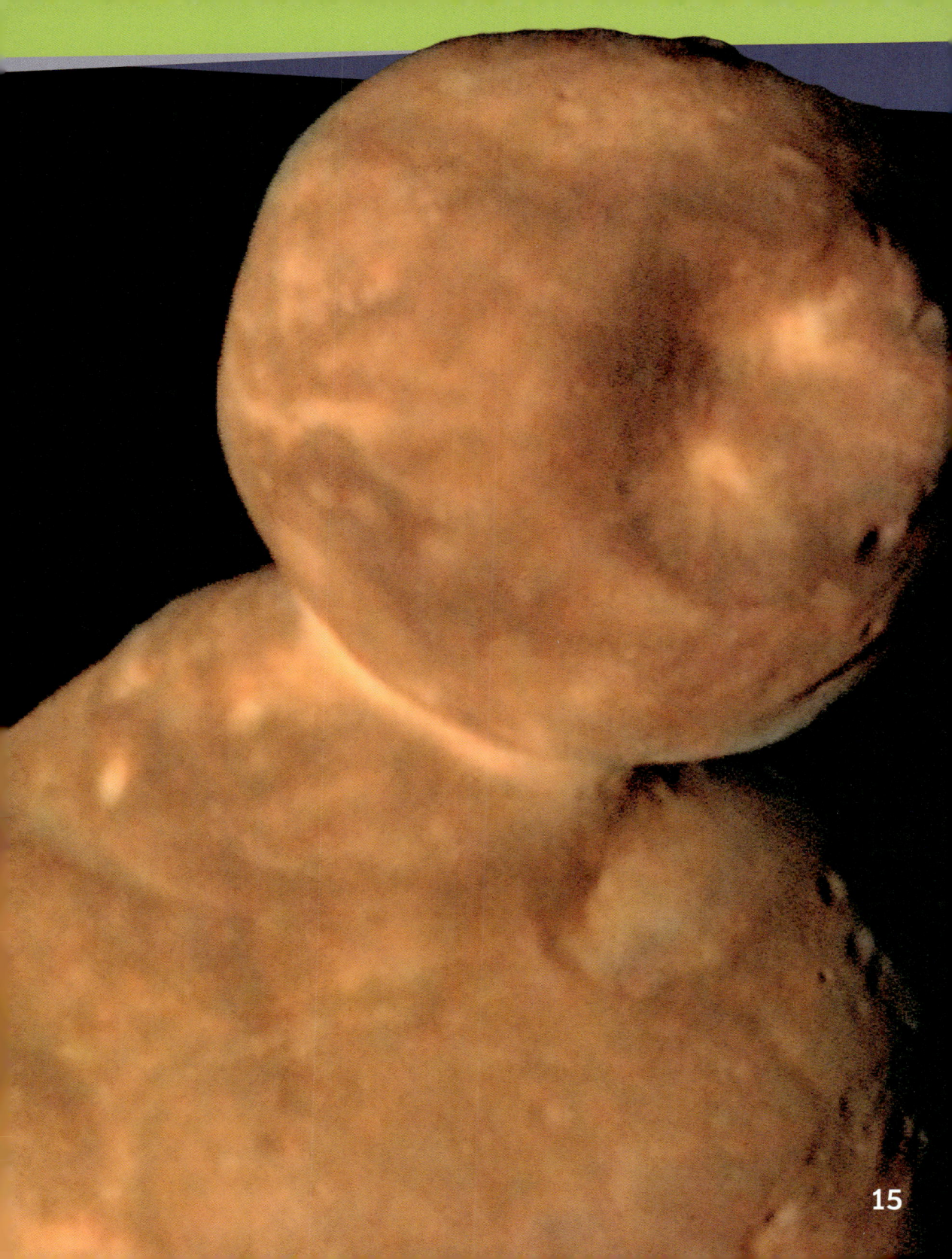

Chapter 3

Space Technology

Technology helps people explore space. For example, rockets lift spacecraft into space. The spacecraft break off from the rockets. Then the spacecraft can travel on their own.

Rockets use huge amounts of fuel when they blast into space.

There are several types of spacecraft. One type is a flyby spacecraft. It passes by an object in space. It gathers data. A second type is an orbiter. This spacecraft travels to the object. Then it slows down quickly. That way, it can orbit the object.

Did You Know?

Some spacecraft shoot probes into comets. The probe smashes into the surface. Then the spacecraft gathers data about the pieces that fly off.

 A spacecraft landed on Saturn's moon Titan in 2005.

A third type of spacecraft is a lander. This type of spacecraft goes to the surface of the object. A lander may carry a rover. This vehicle moves around on the object's surface.

 **An orbiter goes around the same object many times. So, it can learn a lot about the object.**

Some planets are made of gas. Spacecraft cannot land on them. Instead, scientists use atmospheric spacecraft. This type of spacecraft travels toward a planet's center.

It gathers as much data as it can before it is destroyed.

To gather data, spacecraft use instruments. Some instruments might study a planet's soil or rocks. Other instruments gather data from farther away. For instance, many spacecraft use cameras.

Space telescopes also use cameras. Space telescopes are more effective than telescopes on Earth. Space telescopes can gather much more information.

Chapter 4

The Future and Beyond

Space exploration continues every day. Many spacecraft are still going. Some keep traveling farther from Earth. Others orbit planets. They gather more and more data.

 **The Juno probe began orbiting Jupiter in 2016.**

 Scientists work on the Artemis program, which aims to send people to the Moon in the 2020s.

Scientists are working on new projects, too. In 2020, many scientists announced plans. One plan was to return astronauts to the Moon. Another was a new Mars project. A spacecraft would take samples from Mars. It would bring soil and rocks back to Earth.

Scientists were also testing new spacecraft. For instance, scientists often send tiny spacecraft into orbit around Earth. Their small size makes them cost less. As of 2021, no tiny spacecraft had explored deep space. But many scientists were working to change that.

Other scientists were building better instruments. For example, the James Webb Space Telescope entered space in 2021. This space telescope looked at faraway planets. It looked for signs of life.

Scientists have already learned a great deal about space. Even so, many questions still remain.

Did You Know?

The James Webb Space Telescope is 100 times stronger than the Hubble.

 Scientists spent many years developing the James Webb Space Telescope.

For that reason, people will keep exploring space. They will continue to look for answers.

FOCUS ON
Space
Exploration

Write your answers on a separate piece of paper.

1. Summarize the main ideas of Chapter 3.

2. Would you go into space? Why or why not?

3. Which type of spacecraft flies toward the center of a gas planet?

    A. orbiter

    B. lander spacecraft

    C. atmospheric spacecraft

4. Why might tiny spacecraft be able to do riskier projects than large spacecraft?

    A. Tiny spacecraft are much cheaper, so it's less of a problem if the project fails.

    B. Tiny spacecraft are much lighter, so it's easier for them to land on planets.

    C. Tiny spacecraft are much faster, so it's more likely that they will reach space.

5. What does **record** mean in this book?

*Three months later, the probe set a **record**. No spacecraft had ever gone closer to the Sun.*

    A. the best that has ever been done

    B. a way of measuring distance

    C. an object found near the Sun

6. What does **samples** mean in this book?

*A spacecraft would take **samples** from Mars. It would bring soil and rocks back to Earth.*

    A. pictures taken in space

    B. small pieces from a larger object

    C. spacecraft that can land on objects

Answer key on page 32.

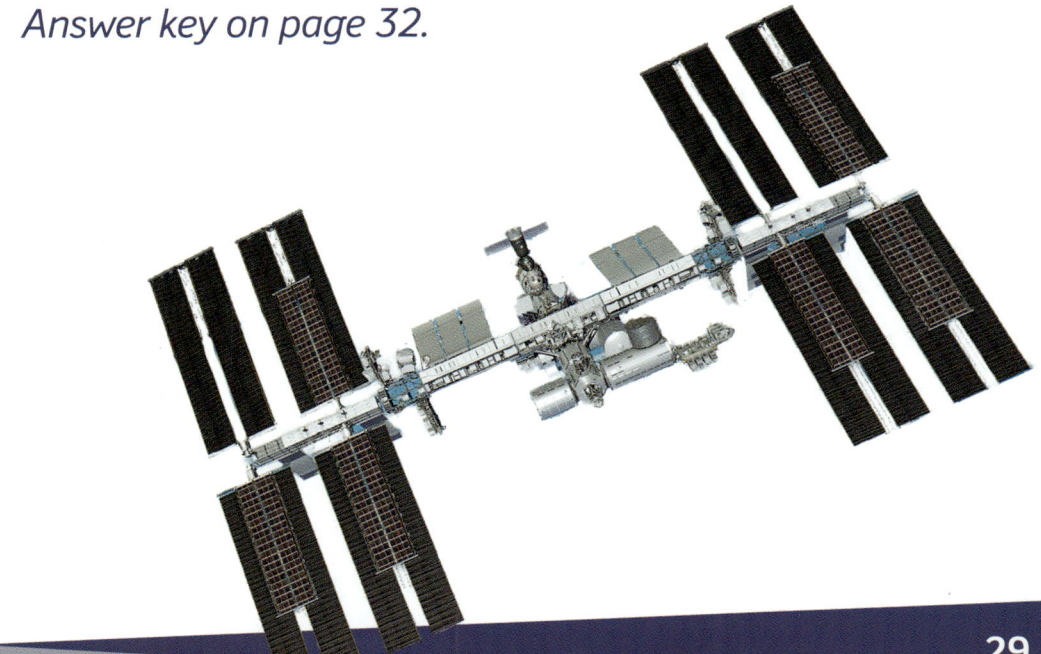

Glossary

astronauts
People who are trained to work or travel in space.

atmosphere
The layers of gases that surround a planet, moon, or star.

data
Information collected to study or track something.

dwarf planet
A ball-shaped object that orbits the Sun but is smaller than a planet.

orbited
Repeatedly followed a curved path around another object because of gravity.

probe
A device used to explore.

rover
A wheeled spacecraft that rolls across the surface of a planet or moon.

solar system
The Sun and all the objects that move around it, including planets, moons, asteroids, and comets.

telescopes
Tools that allow people to see faraway objects.

To Learn More

BOOKS

Collins, Ailynn. *Probe Power: How Space Probes Do What Humans Can't*. North Mankato, MN: Capstone Press, 2020.

Mara, Wil. *Breakthroughs in Space Travel*. Minneapolis: Lerner Publications, 2019.

Mason, Jenny. *Space Exploration: From Galileo Galilei to Neil deGrasse Tyson*. Minneapolis: Abdo Publishing, 2019.

NOTE TO EDUCATORS

Visit **www.focusreaders.com** to find lesson plans, activities, links, and other resources related to this title.

Index

A
asteroids, 12
astronauts, 11–12, 25

D
deep space, 25

H
Hubble Space Telescope, 11, 26

I
International Space Station, 12

J
James Webb Space Telescope, 26

K
Kuiper Belt, 14

M
Mars, 12, 25
Moon, 11, 25

N
Neptune, 11, 14
New Horizons, 14

P
Parker Solar Probe, 5–7
Pluto, 14

R
rockets, 10, 17
rovers, 12, 19

S
solar system, 13
Sun, 5–6

T
telescopes, 9, 11, 21, 26

Answer Key: 1. Answers will vary; **2.** Answers will vary; **3.** C; **4.** A; **5.** A; **6.** B